Cheers! for Thirsty ~~Jane~~ W9-CSX-042

12 Happy Hours

Also by J.K. O'Hanlon

Non-Fiction
3 Ingredient Cocktails

Fiction
Objection Overruled

12 Happy Hours

J.K. O'Hanlon

evenSO Press
Prairie Village, Kansas

Library of Congress Control Number: 2013948936

ISBN 978-0-9882739-4-8

Printed in the United States of America

First Edition

Book design by Mann Made Design • www.mannmadedesign.com
Photo styling by Sonia Spotts of Creative Camp
Editing by Walt Tegtmeier

Quantity discounts are available on bulk purchases of this book. For information, contact evenSO Press, LLC, 3965 West 83rd Street #267, Prairie Village, KS 66208. www.evensopress.com

To
The "Final Friday" neighborhood lushes
and
The "Wednesday Night Gathering" crew

You are my comrades in cocktails, my brothers in booze,
and my sisters in shaking. In other words, you're family.
Thanks for all of the memories and inspiration.

Acknowledgements

The dynamic team that helped me bring *3 Ingredient Cocktails* to press reunited for the production of this book. Once again, they have exceeded all expectations. Lisarae's photography and Sonia's brilliant stylings transport the reader into each month's happy hour. Without Walt and Sally diligently editing, I hate to think what might have made it into print. As usual, Kim pulls it all together in a stunning layout. The team at Kingston Printing always provides top-notch product and service along with an ounce or two of patience. Thanks also go out to Kathie for advising and assisting me in so many ways to transform my dreams into reality. Cheers to Patti and Joel and to Barb and Greg, who graciously allowed us to use their homes for location shots. Kudos to location assistants Daniel and Bria. Many thanks to Uncle Joel for research assistance, not to mention a few drinks here and there. And, saving the best for last, infinite thanks are due to Paul, my partner in life and love, and at the bar. His support and encouragement, not to mention willingness to taste some truly nasty concoctions, which thankfully did not make this book's final cut, are endless and deeply appreciated. I raise my glass to you all!

Table of Contents

Introduction

Gathering with friends, whether on a regular basis, on occasion or spontaneously, creates immediate enjoyment and lifelong relationships and memories. Unfortunately, an unrealistic drive for perfection can paralyze the budding party host, keeping her from breaking out the cocktail shaker and busting out some killer bean dip. Who doesn't want to throw the party of the year? With perfect decorations. A fully stocked bar of exquisite cocktails. A table resplendent with appetizers pretty enough to make a glossy magazine photo shoot. A spotless house. A room full of gorgeous, fascinating revelers dressed to the nines.

About the only thing Thirsty Jane gets right in the above picture is the fascinating guests. After all, aren't friends the real reason to host a party? Okay, maybe your job requires you to throw a party for people you barely like seeing during the day let alone on a Friday night. Perhaps social obligations require an over-the-top presentation. If you find yourself in the position of deep cleaning for people you don't care about, and spending hours in the kitchen slaving over food, perhaps another, fancier book is right for you. There are hundreds of amazing books, blogs, websites and magazines that will help you climb that mountain to being the perfect hostess.

That is not what this book is about.

My first book, *3 Ingredient Cocktails*, empowered the average person to mix a drink with confidence and without breaking the bank. In *12 Happy Hours*, the drink and food recipes and entertaining tips allow you to entertain casually without stress, freeing you up for more fun with your friends.

The concept for *12 Happy Hours* evolved from my two regular cocktail gatherings. One occurs at my home bar on the final Friday of every month (usually). Most people who attend live in the neighborhood, but everyone is encouraged to bring friends, kids and even pets. Another, informally called the Wednesday Night Gathering, is at the home of a friend who once upon a time was just a friend of a friend. A small group of cocktail and liquor aficionados convene every other Wednesday (usually). The group is very diverse in age, occupation and where we live, but we all have some common friendship connection—in addition to our love of cocktails.

In both instances, a core group of individuals makes up most of the parties, with new people and guests attending here and there. Both are regularly scheduled, with set start and end times (more on end times later in November's chapter). Guests usually bring a snack to share, cutting back on the host's obligation. Each gathering also usually features a theme or signature drink, but it devolves from there to beer, wine, or anything in the bar a guest cares to mix.

In neither instance will you find a centerpiece or a spotless house. More than once, my guests have had to run the "Barbie Doll Gauntlet" to reach the bar. If they judge, they don't have to come back! I've never had anyone refuse to return.

If you want to routinely enjoy time with the people you love, in a fun atmosphere with great drinks and easy-to-prepare food, read on. If you want to spend time catching up on your best friend's latest vacation instead of arranging flowers, you have found your book. If you'd rather learn the most interesting secrets about your neighbors—willingly shared and not gossiped, of course—and not sweat over complex appetizers, answers await you within.

Each month contains information that might help with entertaining or simply make you look like a sexy cocktail genius at a party. Three drink and three appetizer recipes follow the month's theme, mood or season. I suggest starting with one signature cocktail for a party and offering a bottle of wine and some beer, along with nonalcoholic beverages. Two huge pitchers of water with glasses nearby grace my bar area at every gathering. You might want to make one appetizer and ask guests to bring a snack to share, if convenient. If you end up with three containers of hummus, smile politely and live with it. No one cares! And no one wants to be micromanaged on what to bring to a casual gathering.

Always remember that the goal of hosting a happy hour is to cultivate friendships and relationships. The food and drink are merely vehicles to relax everyone and get the conversation flowing. If the conversation stalls, and I'm sure it won't, check out some of my ideas in October's chapter for fun and games.

Cheers, and bon appetit!

January

New Year's Resolutions

Almost half of all Americans make New Year's resolutions, but fewer than one in ten actually achieve their goals. That grim statistic might explain why Thirsty Jane has never made a New Year's resolution. Never. Ever. With the odds of failure so high, I suppose that deep down I'm reluctant to put myself out there.

But I appreciate that people use the turning of a year as a time to reassess their lives and resolve to make changes for the better. It's no surprise the number-one resolution made is to lose weight. Great goal! While there are millions of diets and systems "guaranteed" to help you achieve this goal, a dietician once summed up her advice to me: eat less and move more.

Sounds so easy, doesn't it? It's just that implementation opposes me every day around 5 p.m. I love cooking dinner, and I like my cocktails. Over the years, I've become adept at substituting healthier items for the tastier, but fat and calorie laden ones. Cutting back on my cocktail calories presents a trickier challenge.

Because I don't like the taste of artificial sweeteners, the logical choice is to reduce or eliminate the alcohol and its empty calories. These options should please the large number of Thirsty Jane fans who have asked for non-alcoholic options. Of course, you don't need to limit these items to January or to only one party. I encourage you to sprinkle them in with other menus, too. Guests will appreciate having alternatives, and it will keep the party under control.

This month's menu also provides a selection of more healthful appetizers. While I often poke fun at the veggie tray, a good one is both visually stunning and tasty. With this trio of healthful dips, you'll find something to perk up any veggie and satisfy the broccoli-haters in your life.

After losing weight, the second most common resolution is to get organized. Organizing a good happy hour is a micro-version of getting your life more organized. First, decide what type of party you want to host – a sit-down dinner party, casual happy hour or what? Make sure the party goal is realistic. If you live in a studio apartment, a sit-down dinner for 20 probably won't work, but maybe an indoor picnic for 12 will. Finally, set a date and start planning in earnest about four weeks out if this is your first time hosting or the event will be elaborate.

If you've thrown off the shackles of perfection, then pour yourself a non-alcoholic margarita, break out the carrot sticks, and send some texts for a get-together in a few hours.

Non-alcoholic Fizz

A "fizz" is a classic cocktail that can be made with almost any spirit. By substituting a fruit-flavored syrup for the booze, endless non-alcoholic variations abound.

1 ounces fruit flavored syrup*
1/2 ounce lemon or lime juice
4 ounces club soda

Shake fruit syrup with citrus juice and ice. Strain into highball glass filled with ice. Top with club soda. Garnish with mint and/or a piece of fruit that complements the syrup used.

*Look for fruit-flavored syrup at liquor stores, specialty food stores, kitchen stores, and in the beverage section of your grocery store. Monin makes a wide variety of syrups that work wonderfully in non-alcoholic drinks. These are often used to flavor coffee or frozen ice drinks.

Non-alcoholic Margarita

The Margarita is one of Thirsty Jane's favorite drinks, so I shuddered when experimenting with non-alcoholic versions. This one is refreshingly tart and sassy enough even for Thirsty Jane.

1 1/2 ounces fresh lime juice
1/2 ounce orange juice
1 1/2 ounces Thirsty Jane's Sour Mix
Salt (optional)

Moisten rim of a cocktail glass with lime wedge and dip glass in salt. Shake ingredients with ice and strain into cocktail glass filled with ice. Garnish with lime wedge.

Thirsty Jane's Sour Mix

Making sour mix is so simple that you'll never need to buy it again. Plus, this version is much tastier and allows you to control the amount of sweetness and tartness.

1 cup sugar
1 cup water
1 cup fresh lime juice
1 cup fresh lemon juice

Mix sugar and water together in saucepan and heat over medium heat until sugar dissolves and mixture thickens (about 5 minutes). Mix in lime and lemon juice. Let mixture cool. Store in refrigerator.

Non-alcoholic Sangria

Something magical happens when you combine black tea with cinnamon and pomegranate juice. I like using black tea flavored with peach for additional flavor. If you are watching calories, consider using lower sugar juices and a sugar substitute.

2 cups boiling water
2 black tea bags
2 cinnamon sticks
1/2 cup sugar
3 cups pomegranate juice
1 cup orange juice
1 orange, sliced into thin rounds
1 lemon, sliced into thin rounds
1 lime, sliced into thin rounds
3 cups club soda

Pour boiling water over tea bags and cinnamon sticks and steep for 5 minutes. Discard tea bags. Stir in sugar to dissolve. In a large jar or pitcher, combine tea, cinnamon sticks, pomegranate juice, orange juice, orange, lemon, and lime. Refrigerate until cold, preferably overnight. Just before serving, stir in club soda. Serve in glasses over ice.

Trio of Healthy Dips

Different colors, flavors and textures abound in these three dips. Pick your favorite and pair with veggies and/or baked chips.

Curried Yogurt Dip

2/3 cup plain Greek yogurt
1/3 cup low-fat sour cream
1/2 tablespoon curry powder, to taste
1 teaspoon lemon juice
1/4 teaspoon Worcestershire sauce
Salt and pepper, to taste

Combine all ingredients and chill well before serving.

White Bean Dip

1 16-ounce can of cannellini beans, drained and rinsed
2 tablespoons chopped canned jalapeños, to taste (optional)
1 teaspoon chili powder, to taste
1/4 teaspoon cumin
1 tablespoon lemon juice

2 cloves garlic, chopped
2 tablespoons low-fat sour cream
2 tablespoons parsley, chopped
Salt and pepper, to taste

Process all ingredients except parsley in a blender or food processor. Stir in parsley. Chill well before serving.

Avocado Dip

1 cup Greek yogurt
1 ripe avocado peeled, seeded and roughly chopped
2 teaspoons minced canned chipotle chili
2 tablespoons lime juice
2 tablespoons minced cilantro
1 clove garlic, chopped
Salt and pepper, to taste

Mix all ingredients except yogurt, blending with a fork. Stir in yogurt. Chill well before serving.

Baked Chips

These aren't your typical bags of chips, yet they provide an excellent back-drop for your favorite dip and save calories because they are baked not fried. They do tend to lose their crispness quickly, so plan on making them just before your party.

1 package whole-wheat pita bread
1 package corn tortillas
Olive oil spray
Salt

Preheat oven to 350 degrees. Using a knife or pizza cutter, cut the pitas or tortillas into 6 to 8 triangles. For the pita bread, use kitchen shears to separate the two layers of each triangle into separate chips. Lay chips in single layer on baking sheet. Spray with olive oil. Sprinkle with salt. Bake for 10 minutes or until crisp.

Crudités 101

The veggie tray… You want to like it. You want everyone else to like it. Let's face it, though, who wants a carrot dipped in ranch sauce when you can have something, anything, with bacon?

If you are trying to focus on lower-calorie, healthful snacks, the veggie tray is the party queen. Skip the boring ones at the grocery story and do it yourself to groove up the wallflower of appetizer row. Try some of the following choices, in addition to the standards, to bring more color and variety to your crudités:

Asparagus, steamed crisp	Pepper strips
Beet slices, cooked	Radishes
Endive leaves	Kohlrabi strips, blanched
Cucumber slices	Squash or zucchini strips or slices
Green beans, steamed crisp	

Arrange your veggies in a basket or even a clean planter, using cored red or green cabbage as your dip container. Or make a colorful wheel design radiating from a bowl of dip in the center of a platter. The more colorful the options, the more likely you and your guests will reach for a radish or some other fresh, delicious and nutritious snack. New Year's Resolution achieved!

Entertaining Tip:

How Much is Enough?

First, consider how many people will fit comfortably into your space. A good rule of thumb is to ensure five to ten square feet of party space (not your bedroom or bathroom) per guest. Plan on having around 15 appetizer bites per person for a three-hour party. Vary the food and make sure at least one item is substantial. Only you know your how much alcohol your guests usually consume, but two to four drinks over a three-hour party is the average. One 750-ml bottle of spirits makes around 15 drinks. A bottle of wine will provide five servings, and a bottle of champagne serves about six.

February

Show Me The Chocolate

Love, romance, sentimental cards, flowers, and chocolate symbolize Valentine's Day to many. All of these goodies add up, costing the average person well over $100 each year on Valentine's Day. Denying the commercialization of the once-sacred feast day of St. Valentine is futile. But it wasn't always this way. Once it was a holy day and, before that, simply debauchery.

The mid-February celebrations predating the commercial holiday and even the Catholic religious feast day of St. Valentine originate in Rome, where revelers commemorated the empire's founders, as well as the Roman god of agriculture, Faunus. This fertility festival included a sex lottery where men pulled names of mates out of a box. The randomly matched lovers often ended up marrying. Talk about fodder for reality TV!

Hoping to redirect the masses from their depraved carousing, the Catholic Church institutionalized February 14th as St. Valentine's Day in the fifth century. The day commemorates an early Christian martyr named Valentine. Interestingly, three different martyred Valentines hold sainthood, but the Church didn't spell out which one bears the honor of the February 14th feast day. Perhaps the Church's desperation to combat the pagan rituals overrode the need for specificity.

Not until the Middle Ages did the saintly feast day become paired with romance. At the time, people believed February 14th signaled the beginning of the mating season for birds. Riffing on that theme, important historical figures such as Chaucer, the Duke of Orleans, and even King Henry V began sending love notes or poems to their beloved mates.

The romantic traditions continued to blossom until the 1840s, when Esther Howland began selling the first mass-produced valentine cards in the United States. Greeting card giant Hallmark first offered valentine cards in 1913, and then mass production took off only a few years later. Now, more than 150 million cards are exchanged each year. Only Christmas ranks higher.

Yes, receiving a card from a sweetheart warms the heart, and a bouquet of flowers on the desk evidences endearment, but please show me the chocolate! Women love it. I can't explain why, exactly. It's just a fact of life we all live with. What I wonder is, does the guy get the woman chocolate because she loves it or because he thinks it's an aphrodisiac and will enhance the probability of an amorous outcome for the evening?

I own an aphrodisiac cookbook and one chapter concentrates solely on chocolate. I had to know: Is chocolate's love-inspiring power myth or fact? Scientific research confirms that chocolate does contain some chemicals that contribute to feelings of joy or euphoria. For example, tryptophan in chocolate

increases serotonin levels, which can produce feelings of elation. It also contains anadamide, which can also bring about blissful sensations.

Unfortunately, no one has been able to prove that the chemicals in chocolate are strong enough to produce a physiological, sexually stimulating response. Who cares! The stuff is damn good and if eating it makes me feel giddy and playful, then bring it on. For that reason, everything this month features chocolate. Dark, white and in between. Chocolate sweets, chocolate savories, and chocolate salty snacks. Ladies and gentlemen, mix up a cocktail and drizzle some bacon because the night is young!

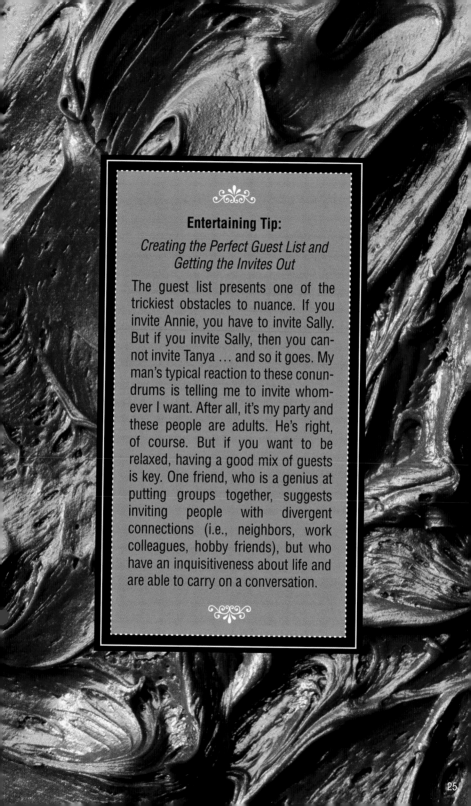

Entertaining Tip:

Creating the Perfect Guest List and Getting the Invites Out

The guest list presents one of the trickiest obstacles to nuance. If you invite Annie, you have to invite Sally. But if you invite Sally, then you cannot invite Tanya ... and so it goes. My man's typical reaction to these conundrums is telling me to invite whomever I want. After all, it's my party and these people are adults. He's right, of course. But if you want to be relaxed, having a good mix of guests is key. One friend, who is a genius at putting groups together, suggests inviting people with divergent connections (i.e., neighbors, work colleagues, hobby friends), but who have an inquisitiveness about life and are able to carry on a conversation.

German Chocolate Cake Cocktail

Chocolate and coconut create a divine combination regardless of the form they take, but especially in a cocktail.

3/4 ounce coconut rum
3/4 ounce dark crème de cacao
1/4 ounce hazelnut liqueur
1 splash half-and-half

Shake with ice and strain into cocktail glass rimmed with cocoa powder.

Chocolate Margarita

This drink satisfies both the tequila lover and questioner in the world. Rich and chocolaty, it defines dessert in a glass. To rim a glass with chocolate, dip the rim in simple syrup and then roll in the very finely chopped chocolate.

1/2 ounce chocolate syrup
2 ounces tequila
1 ounce chocolate liqueur
3/4 ounce half-and-half
1/2 ounce orange liqueur
1 dash almond extract
1 dash ground cinnamon

Shake with ice and strain into cocktail glass rimmed with finely chopped chocolate.

White Chocolate Raspberry Delight

A gorgeous and sweet cocktail, this beauty is also perfect for a bridal shower or girls' night out. Who needs Valentine's Day to celebrate with pretty-in-pink drinks?

1 ounce vodka
1 ounce white chocolate liqueur
1 ounce raspberry liqueur
1/2 ounce white crème de cacao
White chocolate shavings (for rim, optional)

Shake with ice and strain into cocktail glass rimmed with white chocolate shavings. Garnish with fresh raspberry.

Chocolate Macaroons

Choose chocolate to suit your tastes — milk chocolate, semisweet, or bittersweet for those (like Thirsty Jane) who crave the dark side.

7 ounces flaked coconut
2/3 cup sugar
1/3 cup all-purpose flour
1/4 teaspoon salt
3 egg whites
1/2 teaspoon vanilla extract or 1/4 teaspoon almond extract
2 ounces semisweet chocolate, chopped

Preheat oven to 325 degrees. Lightly grease a large cookie sheet or line with parchment paper; set aside. Stir together coconut, sugar, flour, and salt. Stir in egg whites and vanilla extract. Drop coconut mixture by rounded teaspoons 2 inches apart onto the prepared cookie sheet. Bake in the preheated oven for 20 to 25 minutes or until edges are golden brown. Transfer to a wire rack and let cool.

If dipping macaroons, heat chocolate in a double boiler over low heat until melted and smooth. Dip bottom of each cookie in melted chocolate or drizzle melted chocolate over cookies. Place cookies on waxed paper and let stand until set. (Makes about 2 dozen)

Chocolate-Covered Bacon

Chocolate bacon… so wrong it must be right. And it is. Be sure to use the real deal bacon (no low sodium stuff) and opt for the thick cut.

1/2 pound bacon, cut in thirds and fried crisp
1/2 cup semisweet chocolate

Melt chocolate in a double boiler. Drizzle onto bacon strips laid out on waxed paper. Let cool.

Chocolate-Covered Popcorn

Sweet and salty hit the spot with this easy snack. Packaged in cellophane bags with pretty ties, this treat makes the perfect Valentine's Day or hostess gift.

2 quarts popcorn (I use pre-made from local popcorn company)
4 ounces semisweet chocolate

Lay popcorn in single layer on waxed paper. Melt chocolate in a double boiler. Drizzle heavily over popcorn and allow to set. Lay another layer of waxed paper on top of popcorn and flip over. Drizzle chocolate heavily over other side of popcorn. Let set. Break into chunks.

CDARCH

The Saints Come Marching

Oodles of fascinating celebrations pack the month of March. Women's History Month, spring break, and that insane basketball thing that turns the country mad. And don't forget National Crochet Week, plus my favorite, National Frozen Food Month. While chicken nugget appetizers would appeal to my underage fan base, with a name like O'Hanlon, my family would crucify me if this month's theme was not St. Patrick's Day.

But for those of you who closely read my first book, you know that another heritage runs deep in Thirsty Jane's veins. Deep enough to warrant the wearing of folk costumes after a few rounds of vodka shots. Although I cherish my Irish married name, my father gifted me with a last name containing many consonants and few vowels. Yes, my father's family is Polish; my grandfather emigrated from Poland. All this means that I cannot only celebrate St. Patrick's Day. We're also giving a few nods this month to the patron saint of Poland, St. Joseph, whose feast day is March 19th.

St. Paddy, first, because the Irish-inspired drinks are the stars this month. The real St. Patrick lived at the beginning of the fifth century. Born in England, Patrick was kidnapped and taken to Ireland as a child where he worked as a slave. He eventually escaped and, after reuniting with his family, entered the priesthood. Called back to Ireland, he returned to the place of his enslavement with a mission to convert the Irish to Christianity. He worked in Ireland for the remainder of his life.

After his death on March 17, 461 A.D., myths surrounding his life evolved and his status in Ireland as its patron saint emerged. So did he actually drive snakes out of Ireland? Myth. Scientists tell us that snakes never inhabited Ireland. Did he truly use the clover to explain the trinity to the pagan Irish? Maybe, maybe not. But the green clover has become an international symbol of St. Patrick and Irish ethnic pride.

Although March 17th marks the Catholic Church's feast day for St. Patrick, Americans have transformed the day into a secular holiday when everyone wears the green and drinks prodigiously. Who am I to judge about creating excuses for a party? Starting in New York in Revolutionary War times, the Irish and those of Irish heritage came together on March 17th in a show of solidarity. These celebrations spread throughout the country as the Irish immigrant population exploded in the 1800s. Now, even the river runs green in Chicago for St. Paddy's day.

The Irish's successful cohesion in politics and the Catholic Church turned them from underdog to top dog among other ethnic groups at the beginning of the 20th century. Faced with indifferent ears from the Irish-dominated Church, Poles and Italians established neighborhood churches and schools, carrying on their own ethnic traditions.

Both groups celebrated St. Joseph's Day on March 19th, which is the Catholic feast day for St. Joseph, the foster father of Jesus. Italians brought with them a magnificent tradition

of the St. Joseph's Table. Although many legends exist regarding its origins, one of the most common explains that Sicilians facing a severe drought prayed to their patron saint, Joseph, for relief, promising that if he answered their prayers, they would prepare a fabulous feast. The drought broke and the St. Joseph's Table began.

Ethnic Poles in the U.S. adopted the Italian tradition and did their own St. Joseph's Table. The table features a meatless feast that includes beautifully shaped breads and specialty desserts. Many churches and civic organizations sponsoring St. Joseph's Tables will donate food to the needy or collect donations to assist in feeding those less fortunate.

Not to be outdone by the Irish, Poles and Italians wear their red on St. Joseph's Day. Having attended Catholic school in an ethnic Polish neighborhood, do I ever recall the playground battles on March 17th and 19th relating to which color someone wore! Now, I like the attitude that we can all be Irish for a day, and let's say we can also be Polish or Italian for a day, too.

Entertaining Tip:

Feeding the Masses

Prepare one or two appetizers, set out some nuts, and ask guests to bring something to share if convenient. Realistically, you probably don't need every person to bring something, so don't make it feel mandatory for invitees. Stock up on a stack of inexpensive plastic party plates from a discount store or the clearance rack and keep them on hand for parties. Provide plenty of napkins and lots of toothpicks. Have some disposable food containers on hand to send home leftovers with guests in honor of St. Joseph's Day.

Emerald

Does this look familiar? It should. The Emerald, also known as the Paddy, is simply a Manhattan made with Irish whiskey instead of rye.

2 ounces Irish whiskey
1 ounce sweet vermouth
2 dashes Angostura bitter

Stir with ice and strain into cocktail glass. Garnish with maraschino cherry.

Irish Coffee Cocktail

Combine all of the decadence of Irish coffee into a cocktail for this after-dinner drink. Feel free to use instant espresso if you do not have an espresso maker.

1 ounce Irish cream liqueur
1 ounce Irish whiskey
1 ounce espresso

Shake with ice and strain into cocktail glass.

Black Velvet

On St. Patrick's Day, the consumption of Guinness Irish Stout is over double that of any other day of the year! Combine your stout with sparkling wine for a fancier salute to a famous beverage.

4 ounces stout beer
4 ounces sparkling wine

Pour sparkling wine into a champagne flute and top with beer.

Pepper Jelly Cheese Puffs

The savory version of a thumbprint cookie, these foolproof puffs will make you look like a pro in the kitchen. You decide whether to wear your green, red or both.

2 cups sharp cheddar, finely grated
1/2 cup softened butter
1 cup flour
1/2 teaspoon paprika
1 teaspoon salt
Pepper jelly (green for Irish; red for Polish)

Preheat oven to 400 degrees. Combine all ingredients, except jelly, and wrap in plastic. Chill for 30 minutes. Roll into walnut sized balls and put thumbprint in center. Fill with teaspoon of jelly. Bake for 10 minutes.

Green Goddess Dip

This version of the classic Green Goddess dip is lower in fat thanks to the yogurt. The variety of fresh greens gives it a vibrant color and powerful punch of flavor.

2 cups trimmed watercress (about 2 bunches)
1/2 cup fresh basil leaves
1/3 cup mayonnaise
1/4 cup fresh flat-leaf parsley leaves
1/4 cup chopped green onions
1/4 cup plain fat-free Greek yogurt
2 tablespoons olive oil
1 tablespoon white wine vinegar
1 teaspoon anchovy paste
1/2 teaspoon freshly ground black pepper
1/4 teaspoon salt
1/4 teaspoon ground red pepper

Combine all ingredients in a food processor, and pulse 8 to 10 times or until just combined. Chill for 8 hours or overnight. Serve with crackers or veggies.

Candied K

Why settle for little hotdogs in barbeque sauce when you can have Candied K? We're going to overlook the meatless feast part of St. Joseph's Day. You may use a slow cooker for this recipe. Cook on low for 3 hours, uncovering for the last hour.

3 pounds kielbasa sliced into 1/4 inch pieces (like coins)
1 cup packed brown sugar
1/2 cup ketchup
1/4 cup prepared horseradish

Combine in a saucepan and cook over medium heat until mixture boils. Lower heat and cook covered for 30 minutes, then uncover and continue cooking for another hour until the sauce reduces to a thick, sticky coating on the kielbasa, stirring often.

April

Spring Cleaning

When you live in the Midwest, as I do, the idea that spring begins on March 20th invokes snorts of disbelief. Not until after running the April Fool's gauntlet of practical jokes do I permit myself to dream of colorful flowers and sleeping with the windows open. So I've tossed out the vernal equinox as my demarcation of a new beginning and look instead to the month of April for signs of spring.

Throughout the ages, the coming of spring has brought a frenzy of activities inside and outside the home. People throw open windows, let the fresh air circulate, and perform their annual spring cleaning. The ritual's origins remain unclear, but two ancient customs in the Middle East and a more recent and local tradition help explain why spring cleaning exists.

In Iran, where the new year falls on the first day of spring, people "shake the house," meaning clean it from top to bottom to prepare for the new year. Another potential explanation for spring cleaning is the Jewish tradition of cleaning before Passover, which falls in early spring. Because leavened bread may not be present in a household, families clean thoroughly, getting every speck out of the house.

The explanation that makes the most sense to this Midwesterner is that, prior to the invention of the vacuum and central heating systems, homes shut all winter accumulated dirt and grime from wood and coal stoves. Sweeping and airing out the home was impractical given cold climates. When spring's fresh warm breath hit, families would open doors and windows to sweep and air out stuffy and musty quarters. I agree that even with today's conveniences, letting in the first gusts of warm air each spring breathes new life into my home and me.

Over the years, spring cleaning has come to connote more than just thoroughly washing and uncluttering one's home. Office workers might perform a spring cleaning of their files to purge old and unnecessary information and make way for the new tax year. And cocktail aficionados might perform a spring cleaning of their spirits collection to open shelf space for newer, more interesting liqueurs and rid themselves of that Irish cream that has hardened into sludgy goop.

Thankfully, I inherited genes that allow me to discard without distress. Whether it's my closet, kids' papers from school, cards, or that specialty bottle of mustard languishing in the back of the fridge, I use it or lose it. You might call me an anti-hoarder, even. But my liquor collection... I can't throw away that perfectly good, but dusty, bottle of blue raspberry vodka waiting patiently in the back corner for a girls' night out event. Is it perfectly good, though? Do I risk poisoning a guest or just making a bad cocktail if I use that two-year-old crème de menthe? (No arguments allowed on whether crème de menthe ever makes a good cocktail, either. To each her own!)

After researching liquor shelf life and talking to a few industry experts, I think I need to call in my professional organizer friend for an intervention. Or there's going to be one heck of a booze-fest at my house next week. The reality is that some, but not all, liquors last for a very long time. Even indefinitely, some would say. But many of those specialty liquors I've accumulated for swanky cocktails need to go.

How old is too old? Because most distilleries do not include an expiration date on their bottles, the percent of alcohol and the type of flavoring provides general guidance on shelf life. First, most spirits like vodka, rum, tequila, gin and whiskey are at least 40 percent alcohol by volume, or 80 proof. Recall that a spirit's "proof" is always twice the percent of its alcohol by volume. Although some deterioration and evaporation will occur over time, these can be kept indefinitely. If you are using something older than five years, you may want to take a small sample first to ensure the deterioration in flavor isn't too great. Theoretically, high-proof (80 and above) liqueurs should also last indefinitely, but again, take a taste of something more than a few years old.

The tricky choices, especially for booze-hoarders like me, are for those liqueurs between 60 and 80 proof. Examples of these are most of the orange liqueurs and some herbal ones. These should last about two years. Lower-proof liqueurs (between 30 and 60 proof) often have significant sugar in them and tend to deteriorate more quickly. After one year is probably a good time to let go of these. Chocolate, coconut and fruity flavored liqueurs comprise much of this lower-proof category. Cream liqueurs, such as Irish cream, typically last around two years, but check the label and website as these do vary widely. Finally, vermouth needs to be replaced often, about once every month! Essentially, vermouth is wine and it will go bad very quickly.

How to keep track of it all? Put a small sticker on top of a bottle noting when to throw it out. That way you don't have to recalculate the date every time you pick it up. And next time you feel the annual urge to do some spring cleaning, don't forget the bar!

Azalea

Azaleas come in myriad colors, but while living in the South, I fell in love with the deep red variety. This lower-alcohol drink is easy to mix and drink, making it perfect for a spring night on the deck before dinner.

1 ounce Campari
2 ounces pomegranate juice
2 ounces grapefruit juice

Shake with ice. Strain into cocktail glass. Garnish with grapefruit twist.

Entertaining Tip:

Prolonging the Life of Your Booze

No matter what type of alcohol we're talking about, keep the bottles in a stable environment with a cool temperature and minimal exposure to light. Also, always keep the original caps screwed on tightly after use. For sweeter liqueurs, wipe the end of the bottle before sealing to prevent build-up of crystalized sugar. If you have a small amount left of a liqueur, consider transferring it to a smaller bottle to reduce the amount of oxygen available to the contents. Buy little bottles! Unless you have a Manhattan or a wet Martini every night, get the smallest bottle of vermouth. Above all, use common sense. A good friend with an amazing bar admitted that he doesn't hold fast to the shelf life guidelines, although he does agree with them. Use your discretion, but do not let the booze-hoarder make the decision.

Tulip

Don't let the whiskey component intimidate you. One of the most quaffable and interesting drinks I've ever made, this one is perfect for sharing just like a bunch of orange tulips.

2 slices of lemon
2 sprigs of mint
2 ounces rye whiskey
3/4 ounce Aperol
3/4 ounce simple syrup

Muddle lemon and mint in cocktail shaker. Add rest of ingredients and shake with ice. Strain into old-fashioned glass with ice. Garnish with lemon twist and mint.

Daffodil

Sweet and delicate like the first pale yellow flowers of a daffodil, this light and fruity drink takes on added dimensions with the addition of fresh thyme (hopefully from your herb garden!).

1 1/2 ounces vodka
1/2 ounce limoncello
1/2 ounce lime
2 sprigs of thyme

Shake vodka, limoncello, lime and 1 sprig of thyme with ice and strain into cocktail glass. Garnish with other sprig of thyme.

Apricot Brie Wheel

Recycling a classic 80's appetizer.

1 package crescent roll dough
1 jar apricot fruit spread
1 egg, beaten
1 wheel of Brie cheese

Preheat oven to 350 degrees. Lay out 4 crescent rolls to form a square. Spread apricot jam on dough in a circle. Place Brie in the middle and cover with remaining crescent roll dough. Pinch dough together, trimming corners. Brush egg over top. Bake for 20 to 25 minutes. Serve with crackers or sliced French bread.

Fruit Kabobs

Use whatever fruit is in season to make these colorful kabobs. They work well at brunch, too.

Blackberries
Strawberries
Pineapple chunks
Green grapes

Skewer fruit onto bamboo skewers cut to 4 inches in length. Drizzle with Lime Yogurt Sauce.

Lime Yogurt Sauce

This simple sauce is great for dipping, or mixing with your favorite fruit salad to give an old standby some new zip.

1 cup plain yogurt
1 tablespoon honey
1 tablespoon lime juice
1/4 teaspoon grated lime peel

Whisk together.

Deviled Eggs

The trick to a perfectly boiled and peeled egg is to use "older" eggs (about a week old). Add eggs to a saucepan and cover with water. Add in a tablespoon of salt. Bring to a boil, then remove from heat, cover, and let sit for 10 minutes. Plunge eggs into an ice water bath to cool them. Peel under cool running water.

7 large eggs, hard boiled and peeled
1/4 cup mayonnaise
2 teaspoons prepared mustard
1/2 teaspoon seasoned salt
1/4 teaspoon celery seed
Salt and pepper, to taste
Pimentos, for garnishing

Halve 7 eggs lengthwise. Remove yolks and place in a small bowl. Mash yolks with a fork and stir in mayonnaise, mustard and spices. Add salt and pepper to taste. Fill egg whites evenly with yolk mixture. Garnish with pimentos.

MAY

The Mysterious Margarita

Grandma's house was a wonderland for my sister and me growing up. The dining room cabinet housed art supplies that Grandma and Mom always hauled out for us in between marathon Yatzee sessions. The long, skinny yard provided the perfect field for races, all of which I probably lost being the slow-mo runner of the clan. But it was the basement that both intrigued and terrified us.

Beyond the washing machine, water heater and furnace, a tiled area lined with homemade wooden shelves always invited our exploration. It was a mini library, right there in Grandma's basement! Paperback Westerns occupied most of the shelves. Then, there was that "secret" section of Uncle Joe's that we weren't supposed to visit, and never did. I can only imagine! But the rest of the books were pure gold to me -- Agatha Christie mysteries.

Since discovering those books many years ago, a good mystery has always gripped me. I love how, at first, there are no suspects. Then, everyone could have done it. Finally, all of the pieces fall into place and the "whodunit" is revealed. Sadly, after researching the origins of the Margarita cocktail, I feel like I've read an Agatha Christie mystery, only someone has ripped out the last chapter! When it comes to inventing the Margarita, I have no idea who "dun" it.

What's the point of reading about the invention of a drink when there is no definitive story? The point is love, murder, Hollywood starlets, rich Texans, horse racing, and outright messed up mixology comprise the fabric of the Margarita's mysterious past. Although I've read at least 14 different tellings of Margarita's birth, only those most worthy of cocktail party trivia are included here.

Probably the earliest version of the Margarita is a cocktail made in Mexico in the fashion of a "Daisy." A Daisy is simply a type of drink popular in the 1920s and 1930s that consisted of your liquor of choice, orange liqueur, lemon (or lime) juice and a splash of soda. Some reporters stateside described a delicious drink from Mexico: the Tequila Daisy. What's "daisy" translate to in Spanish, inquiring minds might ask? Yep, Margarita.

A bit later in the timeline, a story of improvisation captures my heart because Thirsty Jane is all about improv behind the bar. Bartender Pancho Morales, who slung shots at Tommy's Bar in Juarez, Mexico, received a request for a Magnolia. Stumped (and long before the day of instant internet recipes), Morales did what any O'Hanlon would do – he faked it. He put together tequila, ice, Cointreau, and fruit juice. Bam! Too bad he didn't market his product well. Instead, it's reported that he moved to the U.S. and became a milkman. Moral of the story: embrace your mistakes!

Another of my favorite stories puts Margarita's birth not in Mexico, as most stories do, but in Virginia City, Nevada. Yes, that's the same Virginia City the Cartwright clan from the television series Bonanza frequented! Allegedly, a saloon girl named Margarita took a bullet after instigating a bar brawl with a whiskey bottle over some gunslinger's head. Her beloved, the bartender, invented a drink and named it after her. I like to think that some progeny of Little Joe Cartwright might have been sipping away on a Marg after a day of cattle wrangling and lady killing. But really, does anyone believe this story?

Maybe fictional Old West TV heartthrobs didn't conspire in the invention of America's number one cocktail, but several tales of Margarita's birth do feature Hollywood starlets. One of the more reputable stories revolves around silent screen star Marjorie King. Poor Marjorie was allergic to all alcohol except tequila. Can you imagine that? When imbibing at the Rancho La Gloria Hotel between Tijuana and Rosarito, Mexico, bartender "Danny" Herrera solved Miss King's dilemma by inventing a delectable cocktail comprised of tequila, triple sec and lime juice. He named his invention after Marjorie, giving it a Spanish flair. Bolstering the credibility for this story is the claim from San Diego bartender Albert Hernandez that the owner of La Plaza where he worked knew Herrera and got the idea from him. That Hernandez popularized the Margarita in the U.S. is undisputed. So maybe bragging rights do go to Herrera and starlet Marjorie.

Or do they?

Set your time-travel machine to 1948 and the vacation home of Margaret Sames in Acapulco, Mexico. Sames was a wealthy socialite from Dallas. She wasn't a professional bartender, just enjoyed throwing a great party, not unlike Thirsty Jane! At some point, Sames got tired of the same old same old, and started experimenting with tequila for her guests. Again, sounds a lot like a Friday night at Thirsty Jane's home bar! Eventually, she hit on her preferred ratio: three parts tequila, one part Cointreau, one part lime juice. She called it "The Drink" or "Margarita's Drink." With friends like Nick Hilton (yes, that Hilton) and Hollywood's hottest, Margarita's Drink travelled north to Southern California where it became the rage in the early 1950s.

There's plenty of evidence to suggest that Sames' claim to Margarita fame doesn't hold tequila, but I try not to let the truth get in the way of a good story. So, time to get back to the bar and start shaking because "Juanita's Drink" is ready to be born, and I'm ready to be just as famous as Margaret Sames!

Salud!

Entertaining Tip:

Setting Up the Bar

The key to a successful cocktail party is having drinks available for everyone's tastes without stressing yourself out. Usually, I have beer and a bottle each of red and white wine available for guests who do not like cocktails. Arrange beer and white wine in a bucket or large bowl of ice. Make sure you have a bottle opener and corkscrew handy. Also, always, always have pitchers of ice water and glasses available for guests. Provide washable window markers for guests to write their names on their glasses to avoid mix-ups. Although three drink recipes are provided in each chapter, you might want to mix one signature cocktail per party. Pitchers of drinks are easy, but can also get diluted by melting ice if your guests are slow sippers. Try pre-mixing cocktails and allowing guests to pour over ice in a glass or shaker.

Pineapple-Orange Margaritas

This recipe provides a refreshing alternative to a standard pitcher of Margaritas. If you prefer your Margaritas on the rocks, simply use the juice from the can of pineapple and mix in a pitcher with ice.

1 cup triple sec
1 1/2 cups tequila
Juice from 1 orange
Juice from 2 limes
Sugar to taste
Ice
20-ounce can of pineapple (drained)

Mix all ingredients in a blender. Garnish with zested orange peel.*

*Zested orange peel: Peel orange with vegetable peeler, cutting off white rind. Cut into garnish-sized pieces. Dry for 10-15 minutes and mix with coarse sugar.

ElderRita

Elderflower liqueur has become a hip ingredient with mixologists in the last five years. Here, it gives a swanky feel to a classic Margarita.

1/2 ounce of Elderflower liqueur
2 ounces of tequila
1/2 ounce fresh lime juice

Shake with ice and strain into rocks glass over ice.

Cilantro-Jalapeño Margarita

This Thirsty Jane original perfectly balances sweet, sour and heat. One sampler said, "I could drink 20 of these." Probably not a good idea....

1 tablespoon of cilantro
3 ounces of silver 100% agave tequila
2 ounces triple sec
1 ounce fresh lime juice
3/4 ounce Candied Jalapeño Syrup*

Muddle cilantro in bottom of shaker with lime juice. Add rest of ingredients, shake with ice and strain into a salt-rimmed cocktail glass. Makes either two modest servings or one big, honking serving.

*Available for purchase at specialty stores and online. If you enjoy cooking, try one of the many recipes available online for "Cowboy Candy."

Mango Tostones

Tostones are a common Puerto Rican appetizer and are made from mashed plantains.

1 dozen frozen tostones (substitute frozen potato pancakes)
1 pound pulled pork (buy from deli or pre-made, adding barbeque sauce if meat is plain)
1 mango, diced (fresh if possible, or 1 cup frozen, thawed)
1 tablespoon oil
Fresh chives

Fry tostones in oil. Arrange on plate and top first with warm pulled pork, then the cut-up mangoes. Garnish with chives.

Mexicali Bean Dip

This makes enough for a small army; cut down if planning a small party.

1 can garbanzo beans
1 can black beans
1 can jalapeno pinto beans
1 can black-eyed peas
1/2 cup chopped green pepper
1/2 cup chopped onion
1/2 cup sliced black olives
1 tomato, seeded and chopped
1/2 cup bottled Italian salad dressing
1/2 cup salsa
1/2 teaspoon garlic powder
1 cup shredded cheddar cheese

After draining beans, mix everything together. Serve with tortilla chips.

Fiesta Dip

Disturbingly easy, yet fresh and tasty, and pairs perfect with Margaritas.

8 ounces cream cheese, softened
1/2 cup salsa
4 green onions, sliced thin

Mix all ingredients together. Chill well. Serve with tortilla chips.

June

Gin and Tonic: the Perfect Bond

Nothing cuts through a muggy summer evening like a tall, bracingly cold gin and tonic. G&T's innate pull on me stretches back to those first days of bar hopping when, trying to appear more sophisticated than the beer or rum and Coke drinkers, I followed my big sister's lead down debauchery's path and ordered gin and tonics. Luckily, we drank the good stuff and gin's unique character captivated me. Thank you, Sis. I owe a lifelong love to your introduction.

The gin and tonic's ubiquitous presence at drinking establishments for almost 200 years deserves recognition. How such a simple and elegant cocktail has maintained its staying power over the years is easy to understand because, with only three ingredients and simple proportions, anyone can make this fantastic drink. Its exact origin, however, remains a bit murky, although credit for the drink belongs to the British.

Back in the early 1600s, two unrelated developments occurred that would change the course of cocktails forever. First, the Dutch Courage, also known as genever, found its way across the English Channel where originally it enticed sailors but eventually made its way into aristocratic bars by the end of the century. Gin's popularity exploded into the "Gin Craze" of the 1700s, when much of London spent the day drunk from gin.

Halfway around the world, the Spanish in Peru discovered that the bark of the quina tree cured the fever common in tropical areas. The extract became known as quinine, but the tree from which it was produced was named the "cinchona" after the Spanish Viceroy. Soon, the cinchona became widely used through Europe, including England, to cure fevers.

By the early 1800s, Britain's East India Company solidified its hold in India. Although the potential riches drew the British to the subcontinent, fever from malaria constantly imperiled their continued existence there. Aware of the efficacy of cinchona bark against tropical fevers, Brits combined the bitter bark with sugar and water to improve palatability. At some point in the first quarter of the 19th century, some unknown bloke had the bright idea to further improve the taste of "Indian Tonic Water" by adding a few splashes of Britain's beloved gin. At that time, the rotgut gin that almost proved the ruin of a country had improved in quality and once again graced the sideboards of the elite. That the British officers in India would enjoy gin and make it their alcoholic beverage of choice to combine with the Indian Tonic Water makes sense.

So far, all of this seems perfectly rational to me. Instead of a morning medicinal, those with access to the good booze simply took their mosquito fever prophylactic in the evening with a tipple of gin. The Indian Tonic Water they used was not the fizzy tonic used today, however. For that invention, credit lies with the mysterious Bond, Erasmus Bond, that is. Building upon the British military officer's habit of taking gin with a "tonic," Erasmus Bond patented a new and improved tonic water. The innovation? Bubbles!

The effervescent tonic combined with gin produced a delightful summer drink in England for those returned from India and their friends. Soon, others copied the concept and the Schweppes company debuted its own form of fizzy tonic water in the 1870s. From there, not much is written about the glorious gin and tonic. People continued to enjoy its medicinal effects until World War II when artificial quinine was developed after the Japanese took control of Indonesia, where most of the world's cinchona grew. Since then, most commercially produced tonic water contains only small amounts of quinine. Now, with the craft cocktail mania, small companies are once again producing tonic water with cinchona bark and cane sugar. This fact gives me great confidence as I set out into my mosquito-infested yard.

Although Erasmus Bond received his tonic water patent on May 28, 1858, my guess is that with the speed of the British post, it was probably June before he held that paper and was ready to embark on his new adventure.

The month of June should therefore celebrate not only great gin but also the bubbly stuff that makes it all the better. Pour yourself some gin with twice the amount of tonic water and as much ice as possible. Add a lime squeeze or, if you are like the other famous Mr. Bond, make it a double and use the entire lime. I'd write more, but there's a drink beckoning and it's called the gin and tonic.

DIY G&T Bar

Lay out in a cafeteria line style:

Ice in bucket with scoop

High ball glasses

Variety of gins
   Try: traditional London dry gin, Plymouth gin, floral and botanicals gins

Variety of tonics
   Try: standard tonics as well as some of the craft tonics made
   with cinchona

Variety of liquor embellishments
   Try: Campari, crème de cassis, elderflower liqueur, crème de violette

Variety of fruit and veggie embellishments
   Try: lime, lemon, orange, grapefruit, cucumber, mint, basil, rosemary

Variety of bitters
   Try: lemon, lime, rhubarb, celery

Index cards and pens to memorialize winner recipes

Provide instructions at each stop for guests. I use small chalkboards.

1. Fill glass with ice

2. Pick your poison (add 2 ounces of gin)

3. Pick your medicinal (add 4 ounces of tonic)

4. Embellish using your imagination

5. Write down a good drink!

You may want to provide guests with some examples of winning combinations. Some of the best from a recent DIY event at Thirsty Jane's bar are:

- Gin, tonic, 2 dashes Peychaud's bitters, 2 dashes Angostura bitter, squeeze of lime, squeeze of grapefruit

- Gin, tonic, 1/2 ounce crème de violette, 2 dashes orange bitters, mint sprig and orange slice

- Gin, tonic, 1/2 ounce elderflower liqueur, squeeze of grapefruit

- Gin, tonic, muddled cucumber and rosemary, 1 dash celery bitters

Cucumber Canapés

Like a good G&T, this appetizer is refreshing, simple and works all summer.

1 cucumber, sliced into 1/4 inch pieces
Boursin cheese
Grape tomatoes, sliced in half
Sea salt

Spread thin layer of Boursin cheese on each cucumber slice. Top with 1/2 grape tomato. Sprinkle with sea salt.

Seafood Wraps

My friend Nate captains the Marauder Sailing Charter company in Vieques, Puerto Rico, and provides the most amazing lunches and appetizers aboard his cruises. This recipe pleases everyone!

3-4 large spinach wraps
8 ounces of cream cheese, softened
1 teaspoon minced garlic
1 tablespoon butter
1 pound frozen salad shrimp, thawed
4 green onions, sliced
2 tablespoons fresh dill, chopped

Sauté garlic in melted butter. Add shrimp and warm, then let cool. Mix cheese with chopped onion, herbs, salt and pepper to taste. Mix in cooled seafood. Lay out wrap on cutting board and spread mixture evenly around the entire wrap. Be generous, it should be about ¼-inch thick. Next, roll it like a jelly roll. Slice ½- to ¾-inch pieces on a diagonal. Refrigerate until ready to serve.

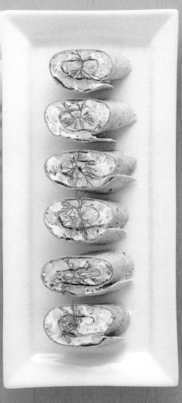

Thai Peanut Dip with Green Beans

With this dip, you will eat several servings of vegetables. I like blanched green beans, but try asparagus or any other veggie you have handy. To blanch green beans, put them in boiling water for two minutes and then plunge them into an ice bath. Remove and refrigerate until ready to serve.

1 cup roasted peanuts
5 ounces chili sauce
Juice from 1/2 lime
1/4 to 1/3 cup hot water

Pulse peanuts in food processor until roughly chopped. Add in chili sauce and lime juice and hot water by drops and continue pulsing mixture until the consistency of a dip. Serve alongside blanched and chilled green beans.

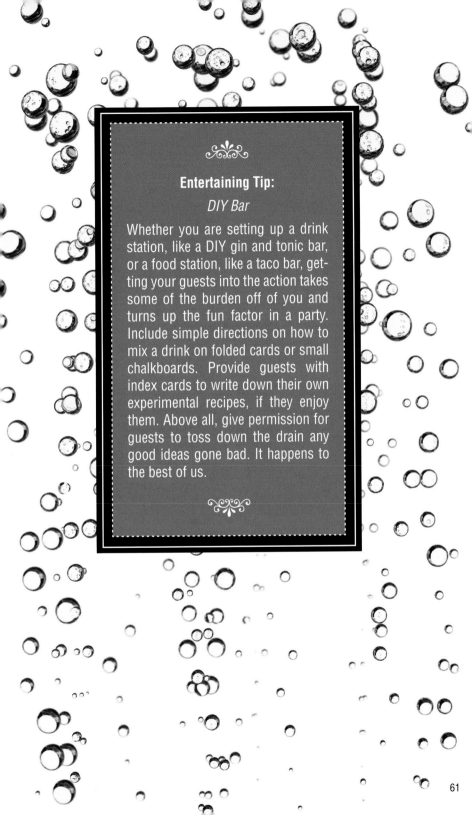

Entertaining Tip:

DIY Bar

Whether you are setting up a drink station, like a DIY gin and tonic bar, or a food station, like a taco bar, getting your guests into the action takes some of the burden off of you and turns up the fun factor in a party. Include simple directions on how to mix a drink on folded cards or small chalkboards. Provide guests with index cards to write down their own experimental recipes, if they enjoy them. Above all, give permission for guests to toss down the drain any good ideas gone bad. It happens to the best of us.

July

Cocktailing Colonials

For anyone who thinks the founding fathers exhibited superior moral fiber, at least in the alcohol consumption category, the truth about Colonials' prodigious drinking is startling. According to the Colonial Williamsburg Foundation, in each year of the 1790s, individuals over the age of 15 consumed over 30 gallons of cider and beer, five gallons of distilled spirits, plus about a gallon of wine. Now, the National Institutes of Health reports that average annual consumption of beer is just over a gallon, a bit under a gallon for spirits and less than half a gallon for wine. Of course, in Colonial times, beer and cider came in both low and high alcohol versions. Still, the thought of consuming that much alcohol turns my stomach queasy, especially when thinking about the common early morning pick-me-ups with which Colonialists partook.

Yes, drinking was an all-day affair for the early Americans. The daybreak libation consisting of spirits, sugar and water resembled what we now call a cocktail. Although the term "cocktail" wasn't used until the 1800s, it may have originated from this Colonial practice. Quaffing continued throughout the day, whether at home, work or school. Because the raw materials for cider and beer grew in abundance, and the process for brewing proved simple, most homes produced their own brews. "Small" beer's lower alcohol content made it the drink of choice for children and servants.

Even teetotalers accepted drinking low-alcohol beer and cider. Their complaints about abuse of alcohol related to distilled spirits only. The difference stems back to bad water in Europe. Because water boils during the brewing process, the contaminated European waters became safe to drink when brewed into ale or cider. However, America's water supply in the 1700s was extremely clean. Yet people still feared becoming sick and chose to hydrate with the low-alcohol home brews.

Throwing out the Colonial beer-guzzling statistic, early Americans nonetheless put the hard liquor away! Two spirits, rum and whiskey, played important roles in the fledgling country's history. Pre-Revolutionary War, rum held title as the hard spirit of choice. Caribbean sugar plantations exported molasses to the British Colonies where rum distilleries proliferated, every major town having its own production facility. By 1770, well over 100 distilleries produced nearly 5 million gallons of rum annually. Although inferior to the Caribbean-produced rum, the cheap American versions satisfied Colonists and supplied trade to Europe and Africa, becoming an integral part of the horrific slave-trafficking business.

During the Revolution, disruption of the shipping routes drastically reduced rum production. Americans turned to homegrown raw materials of corn and rye and ramped up production of whiskey. Immigration of Scotch-Irish to the mid-Atlantic states brought a breadth of knowledge relating to distillation of whiskey. George

Washington recognized the potential in the new spirit and installed a distillery at Mount Vernon. According to Mount Vernon historians, the five stills produced more than 10,000 gallons of whiskey by the end of the 18th century, making Washington one of the country's largest distillers at the time of his death.

One of the ways Colonists consumed their rum and even their whiskey was in punch. Punch originated in another colony of the British Empire, India, before making its way to America. Although recipes for and variations on particular recipes abound, punch essentially includes spirits (usually some combination of rum, brandy and/or Madeira), water, lemons or limes, sugar and spices. Particularly in the South, punch slaked the thirst of landowners who rubbed elbows plotting revolution. Truly a historic beverage, punch encourages friends to gather round the big bowl for an evening of conviviality. A plus for a host is that she only has to make the drink once! What could be simpler?

Jane and Jerry's Gin Punch

Most punches are rum-based, with brandy or whiskey added. Being a gin lover at heart, I wanted to include a gin punch. "Professor" Jerry Thomas, the father of the American cocktail, included a few gin punch recipes in his 1862 book. This is my variation on one of them.

1 750 ml bottle of gin
4 ounces raspberry liqueur
12 ounces pineapple juice
6 ounces lemon juice
2 lemons, sliced
2 limes, sliced
2 oranges, sliced
1/2 pineapple cut into chunks
1 pint raspberries
1 liter club soda

Combine all ingredients but club soda in a container and refrigerate until cold. Just before serving, add club soda and a decorative ice block.

Martha Washington's Rum Punch

This recipe supposedly comes from the First Lady's personal notes. Whether that's truth or urban myth doesn't matter. This traditional planter's punch features the typical sour, sweet, strong and weak (citrus, sugar, spirits, water).

4 ounces lemon juice
4 ounces orange juice

4 ounces simple syrup
3 lemons quartered
1 orange quartered
1/2 teaspoon grated nutmeg
3 cinnamon sticks broken
6 cloves
12 ounces boiling water

In a large bowl, mash lemons, orange, nutmeg, cinnamon sticks and cloves. Add syrup, lemon and orange juices. Pour boiling water over the mixture. Let cool. Strain out solids. Heat juice mixture to a boil and simmer for 10 minutes. Let cool and refrigerate overnight.

In a punch bowl, combine:
3 parts juice mixture
1 part light rum
1 part dark rum
1/2 part orange curaçao or triple sec

Serve punch over ice. Top with grated nutmeg and cinnamon.

Admiral Schley's Punch

Unlike many punches, this one can be prepared individually and consists of readily available spirits. The drink's namesake, Winfield Scott Schley, held the rank of Admiral in the U.S. Navy and commanded ships during the Spanish-American War at the end of the 19th century.

1 ounce dark rum
1 ounce bourbon
1 teaspoon sugar
Juice and peel from 1 lime

Combine all ingredients with ice in a shaker and shake vigorously. Pour into a glass and garnish with mint and pineapple.

Spiced Pecans

Despite the cayenne, these nuts do not hold significant fire. Increase cayenne if you like it hot!

1 teaspoon salt
3/4 teaspoon freshly ground black pepper
1/2 teaspoon cayenne pepper, to taste
1 1/2 teaspoons ground cinnamon
1 1/2 tablespoons light brown sugar

1 pound pecan halves
4 tablespoons unsalted butter, melted

Preheat oven to 350 degrees. In a small bowl, combine salt, black pepper, cayenne, cinnamon and brown sugar. Spread the pecans on a large, rimmed baking sheet and toast for 8 to 10 minutes, until fragrant. Transfer pecans to a large bowl and toss with butter. Add spices and toss to coat. Return pecans to baking sheet and toast for 3 to 4 minutes longer, until fragrant. Let cool.

Ham Biscuits

Having gone to school in the South, I know the ham biscuit is a ubiquitous part of any buffet.

1 1/2 pounds Virginia ham (buy thick sliced at the deli or go whole hog and cook yourself a Virginia ham for a true adventure)

24 biscuits

Cut apart biscuits and place a few slices of ham on each. Serve with assorted mustards.

Southern-style Biscuits

Feel free to use your own recipe, or in a pinch, get the premade biscuits in a can from the grocery store, but try the following for easy Southern-style biscuits.

2 cups self-rising flour
1 cup shortening, chilled
2/3 to 3/4 cups buttermilk
2 tablespoons melted butter

Preheat oven to 450 degrees. Coat baking sheet with no-stick cooking spray. Cut shortening into flour using a pastry blender or 2 knives until crumbs are the size of peas. Blend in just enough milk with fork until dough leaves sides of bowl. Turn dough onto lightly floured surface and knead gently 2 to 3 times. Roll dough to 1/2-inch thickness. Cut using floured 2-inch biscuit cutter. Place 1 inch apart on prepared baking sheet, or almost touching for soft sides. Brush melted butter over tops of biscuits. Bake 8 to 10 minutes or until golden brown.

Cheese Straws

Don't let the food processor or thought of working with dough intimidate you. If you don't own a food processor, blend with a fork or pastry blender. This dough is fool-proof and the end product will impress your guests. Caution: These are highly addictive!

1 1/2 cups grated extra-sharp cheddar
1 cup all-purpose flour
3/4 stick cold unsalted butter, cut into tablespoons
1/2 teaspoon salt
1/8 teaspoon cayenne
1 1/2 tablespoons milk

Preheat oven to 350 degrees. Pulse cheese, flour, butter, salt and cayenne in a food processor until mixture resembles coarse meal. Add milk and pulse until dough forms a shaggy ball. Roll out dough on a lightly floured surface with lightly floured rolling pin into a 12- by 10-inch rectangle (about 1/8-inch thick). Cut dough with a lightly floured pizza wheel or lightly floured sharp knife into 1/4-inch-wide strips. Carefully transfer to ungreased baking sheets, arranging strips 1/4 inch apart. Bake 15 to 18 minutes, until golden brown. Cool completely on baking sheets on racks. Serve with pepper jelly for an added kick.

Entertaining Tip:

Dealing with Outdoor Issues

Maybe Colonials didn't care about bugs and rain, but today either can threaten to derail any outdoor party. If you want to entertain outdoors and are not hosting spontaneously, make sure you have space inside if the weather turns inclement, like when the tornado came through the night of the outdoor rehearsal dinner I hosted (mine, by the way). For bugs, natural tips to evade their menace include serving food inside, covering outdoor food with mesh colanders, keeping food and drink stations away from shrubs and flowers, cleaning any standing water in ponds, birdbaths, etc., removing empty drink glasses ASAP, and ensuring a breeze is nearby by placing a fan outside.

August

End of Summer Blues

Whether sending kids back to school or stowing your white shoes in the closet until next Memorial Day, the end of summer marks the passage of time like the chimes on a grandfather clock. The time for vacation and being just a little more laid-back behind, the blues set in at this point every year for me.

Confronting end of summer melancholy by toasting with a blue menu may not cure a downcast mood, but hosting a party with summery drinks allows the savoring of the season to last another night.

Making your drink blue requires both care and a high risk-tolerance for the same reason: blue food and drink aren't normal. Some might even say they're an abomination. Call me crazy or just inclusive, but a bright blue drink turns me on. It takes my thoughts to a Caribbean island. From there, I'm a goner imagining curling my toes in the warm sand and sipping a vividly colored fruity drink from a perfectly sweaty glass. For others, though, the unnatural color triggers a visceral reaction that the food or drink must be tainted to have that lurid color.

Assuming you are ready and willing to take the risk that friends will not rebuff your carefully crafted cocktails, how can you create that shockingly electric color? A handful of blue-colored liqueurs exist, many being branded variations of fruit-flavored vodka.

The more versatile and readily available option is blue curacao. Essentially, it is blue-colored orange curaçao, an orange-flavored liqueur similar to

triple sec. For everything from a Margarita to a Kamikaze, substitute blue curaçao for triple sec and your drink instantly becomes lively and exciting.

So exciting that some partake too liberally, which leads to the second reason a guest might shun your blue piece of paradise. More than a few friends balk at my penchant for blue drinks because of "that night" years or even decades ago when they overindulged. You'll know who they are after hosting a party with blue-hued beverages. For them, have an alternative on hand, which is a good idea in any circumstance.

Back to the blue liqueurs. Admittedly, the difference between curaçao, triple sec, and the brands Cointreau and Grand Marnier still confound me. No expert or resource has been able to definitively clarify the differences. Part of the problem is that, like many liqueurs, no standard exists defining what is curaçao and what is triple sec.

Curaçao originated on the Caribbean island of Curaçao where Spanish settlers planted Valencia orange trees. Unfortunately for the settlers, but fortunately for cocktailers, Curaçao's climate didn't favor the Valencia orange and a bitter small orange evolved called the laraha.

Distillers take the bitter peel from the laraha and dry it before soaking it in water and alcohol. After removing the peel, the distiller adds spices and the spirit is distilled. Curaçao first appeared in the 1880s after the Dutch had taken control of Curaçao.

France answered the Dutch's new liqueur with their own "triple sec" or a triple-distilled version. Cointreau and Grand Marnier are simply types of higher-end triple sec. Because Grand Marnier uses brandy as its base, like the traditional curaçao, some say that it resembles curaçao more closely than triple sec.

The bottom line is that all are orange-flavored liqueurs, but alcohol content and quality will vary across brands. For all of the end of summer blue drinks, nothing specific in the blue curaçao variety is required. Stop sweating the details and enjoy another day of hanging out, or at least another night.

An alternative way to use your newly acquired blue-blooded cocktails is for a Once in a Blue Moon Party. A "blue moon" is the second full moon in a calendar month. This occurs only once every two to three years; hence, the saying "once in a blue moon" signifies something that rarely happens. If your happy hour falls on a blue moon, throw out all plans and reach for the blue curaçao because such a rare event deserves a celebration.

Entertaining Tip:

Party Flow and Setup

Set your drinks and food in different locations to encourage guests to move about. Put napkins and utensils at the end of a buffet line so guests don't have to juggle them when loading up their plates. Move coffee tables and end tables to other rooms to open the area. Five or 6 people sitting in your living room talking across tables isn't inviting to other guests and can be difficult once the party gets rolling. Your goal is to have people walking around and mingling, which is easier in an open space. Although coats may not be an issue in August, for other times of the year, empty your coat closet for the night or designate a bed or bench for guests to deposit coats and purses.

Beach Bum Redux

The summer's over and your beach chair has been hung up in the garage. This drink will take you back to warm days by the pool. Think Piña Colada, only better. If you don't want to get out the blender, shake together and pour over ice in a highball glass.

1/2 ounce crème de banane
1/2 ounce blue curaçao
1/2 ounce coconut rum
1 ounce pineapple juice

Blend in a blender with ice and pour into hurricane glass. Garnish with umbrella.

Mother Jane's Ruin

In 18th century England, gin carried the label "Mother's Ruin" because of its effects on families from the corrupting overindulgence. This tasty concoction could easily become Thirsty Jane's ruin!

2 ounces gin
1 ounce blue curaçao
1 teaspoon peach schnapps
1/2 ounce lime juice

Shake with ice and strain into cocktail glass. Garnish with a peach slice.

Blue Lagoon

A no-brainer for the end of summer blues, this drink is refreshing and light.

2 ounces vodka
1 ounce blue curaçao
3 ounces lemonade

Pour into highball glass filled with ice. Stir. Garnish with lemon wheel.

Blue Cheese Pizza

You have to love blue cheese to like this one, but if you are a fan of the blue-veined stuff, this appetizer will not disappoint.

2 pieces of Naan bread
Blue cheese dressing
1/4 cup grated Parmesan cheese
1/2 pound bacon, chopped and cooked
4 ounces blue cheese crumbles
1 bunch green onions, white parts thinly sliced

Preheat oven to 350 degrees. Spread dressing onto crust. Sprinkle with blue cheese crumbles, green onions, Parmesan and bacon. Bake for 15 to 20 minutes.

Peanut Butter Bacon Stuffed Dates

So entirely wrong, but deliciously right. Do not make these if you are home alone!

Dates
Peanut butter
Bacon fried crispy and cut into 1-inch pieces

Slit open dates (removing pits if necessary). Fill with 1/2 teaspoon of peanut butter and insert piece of bacon.

Beach Pinchos

Pinchos originated in Spain, but the Puerto Rican version, found at many roadside vendors, consists of only meat on a skewer. This particular sweet and smoky variation comes from a friend in Puerto Rico.

2 chicken breasts, cut into 1-inch cubes
1/4 cup honey
1 tablespoon sweetened coconut
1/8 teaspoon mesquite liquid smoke
1/8 teaspoon cayenne pepper
Salt
Pepper

Combine all ingredients. Let chicken marinate for at least 2 hours. Skewer 3 pieces of chicken onto shortened bamboo skewer. Grill for 5 minutes over medium heat. Turn and baste with marinade and grill for another 5 minutes. Be careful not to overcook or chicken will be dry and tough.

September

An Apple (Drink) A Day…

For me, September means back to school, football, and a trip to the apple orchard for cider and dough-nuts. Cooler weather begs for apple pies, apple tarts, apple crisps, apple muf-fins, apple cake and apple cobblers. Did I mention cider doughnuts already?

Between the abundant selection of apple types and the comeback of some heritage varietals, an apple exists for every taste and use. Admittedly, every year the urge to gorge overcomes me, and within a few weeks I'm appled-out. If only I'd listened to my dear father, the master of maxims, who advised that one apple each day would indeed keep the doctor away.

Seriously?!

Common sense dictates that because it's a fruit, an apple surely possesses plentiful nutrients essential to a healthy body. And my elemental grasp on logic suggests that if an apple is good for me, then apple juice must be good for me, and that means apple cocktails are good for me! I'm not that naïve, so back to the original question, can a daily apple ward off illness?

Multiple studies have examined the health effects of apples. Indeed, they do pack some serious firepower in the nutrient department. Their low-caloric density makes them a perfect snack for people looking to slim down. In other words, an apple pro-vides a substantial amount of food for the low calorie and high fiber content. This keeps the apple-snacker full longer than the same amount of calories in a sugary or refined grain-based snack. Also, studies have linked apples to lower cholesterol, better lung function, boosted immunity, and a decreased risk of diabetes. And they clean your teeth! Additionally, apples are easy to grow, readily available from local orchards in many parts of the country, inexpensive and delicious.

If apples supply so many health benefits, doesn't apple juice or cider do the same thing? Unfortunately, most of the super-hero chemicals in apples are in the skin. The process of making apple cider and apple juice removes most of the health effects. To make cider, apples are washed, cut and mashed. A press then squeezes the juice from the mashed up apples. The resulting liquid is apple cider. The bulk of production occurs in fall, when the crops come in, and many cider makers use particular varieties to give their product a distinctive taste. Most cider is now pasteurized for longer shelf life, but you're still looking at only a few weeks for prime cider buying. Apple juice takes cider a step further. Filtration removes the particles to create the clear, golden juice. Vacuum sealing in addition to pasteurization extends the shelf life considerably.

Apple cider changes character quickly after the bottle is opened. The natural yeasts will begin to ferment even in refrigerated cider, creating a very unappetizing and possibly unsafe brew after a while. Brewers continue the fermentation process to produce "hard" cider. Except in the United States, "cider" means the alcoholic version, typically containing about 5 percent alcohol by volume. Bubbly and tangy, hard cider is an acquired taste.

Other alcoholic uses for apples are as brandy, applejack and schnapps. Like so many liquors I've researched, what specifically differentiates one from another based upon ingredients and/or distillation methods isn't exact with these spirits, except for calvados, a French apple brandy, which is tightly controlled. All of this leads me to the question, is apple schnapps just a German version of apple

brandy? And isn't schnapps the sickeningly sweet stuff someone you know (maybe you) got drunk on at an inappropriately early age?

In Germany and Austria, where schnapps in a wide range of flavors is popular, the liquor is fruit brandy, which simply means the fruit is fermented and then distilled. Unlike French apple brandy, German apple schnapps is not aged and remains clear. The American version of schnapps is more of a liqueur because the fruit juices are blended with a neutral distilled spirit. Sugar and coloring may be added. The result is a sweeter spirit, lower in alcohol. Undoubtedly, this type of apple a day is not going to keep the doctor away.

Where did that saying come from, anyway? Apparently, it is an old Welsh proverb that originally went something like this: "Eat an apple on going to bed, and you'll keep the doctor from earning his bread."

Maybe, maybe not. Eating an apple every day cannot hurt, but don't be so enthusiastic about this month's spirited apple libations!

Entertaining Tip:

Ambiance Through Lighting and Music

People come to a party to have fun, which means great conversation, drinks and food. While stunning decor is appreciated, it is seldom remembered, so keep it simple and stress free. Candles are perfect for an evening fete. And when I say candles, I mean lots of candles. Everywhere. Simple, inexpensive tea lights or votives are perfect. Background music helps, especially in those first 15 minutes of a party before the crowd rolls in and chatter picks up. Enlist a friend to be in charge of music, keeping the volume level right and dealing with any breaks in the tunes. Finally, if you're going to go for flowers, pick up one huge bunch of big flowers at the local market and put in a plain vase for a bold statement.

Apple Spice Cocktail

Everything in this drink is delicious, so no surprise that the combination results in liquid autumn. Run a lemon wedge around the rim of the glass before dipping into a cinnamon sugar mix to obtain the perfect rim.

2 1/2 ounces golden rum
2 ounces apple juice
Splash amaretto

Shake with ice and strain into cocktail glass rimmed with cinnamon sugar mix.

Northern Apple

Called the "Northern Apple" because of the use of Canadian whiskey, this drink is smooth, full and flavorful. Both whiskey fans, and those who fear the dark spirits, enthusiastically approved of this cocktail. Be sure to use apple schnapps (or apple liqueur) and not anything labeled sour apple.

1 1/2 ounces Canadian whiskey
1 ounce apple schnapps
2 ounces cranberry juice

Shake with ice and strain into cocktail glass. Garnish with red apple slice.

Cran-Apple Cobbler

A "cobbler" can be both a dessert and a vintage cocktail, usually made with wine, sugar, shaved ice and fruit. This drink resembles the dessert. Although not overly sweet, the combination of spirits with the graham cracker rim imitates a favorite fall treat. To get the graham crackers to stick, dip the glass in simple syrup and then into finely crushed crackers.

2 ounces vodka
1 ounce cranberry juice
1 ounce apple cider
1/2 ounce lemon juice

Shake with ice and strain into cocktail glass rimmed with crushed graham crackers.

Hot Bacon and Cheese Dip

It's the mother lode of cheese and bacon dip. Eat it up while warm to enjoy the fluffy consistency of the cheese.

8 ounces cream cheese
1/2 cup mayonnaise
4 ounces shredded Swiss cheese
6 slices cooked bacon, cut into bite-sized pieces

In a microwave safe dish, add first three ingredients and cook on high for 4-5 minutes, stirring halfway through, until creamy. Sprinkle bacon on top and cook for another minute. Serve with crackers.

Spiced Marcona Almonds

The No. 1 pick of my taste-testers, these highly addictive almonds might cause bar fights!

1 pound roasted marcona almonds
2 teaspoons olive oil
2 tablespoons minced fresh thyme leaves
1 teaspoon salt

Preheat oven to 350 degrees. Combine all ingredients in a bowl and mix well. Place on cookie sheet and bake in oven for 10-15 minutes turning regularly, until lightly brown. Cool completely.

Shrimp Cocktail Shooters

The "count" for shrimp represents the number of shrimp typically found in one pound. Slightly larger shrimp work well in this recipe if you can find them at your grocer.

1 pound 15-16 count shrimp
1 cup cocktail sauce
1/2 tablespoon wasabi paste
Fresh chives

Peel and devein shrimp, leaving tail on. Steam shrimp, cooling with ice after cooked. Mix cocktail sauce and wasabi. Spoon cocktail sauce into shot glass, add in shrimp and a few chives to stick up.

October

Tricks, Treats, and Toasts to the Zombie Apocalypse

Halloween ceased to be an official candy-gathering recon mission when I turned 13, but the fun has never ended for me or the vast majority of Americans who participate in Halloween, whether dressing up, handing out candy, attending a party, or all of the above. And while my days of mapping out the neighborhood like a black ops unit leader are over, I still practice stealth getting the stuff out of the candy bowl and my kids' bags without being caught. Judge not, for I'm not alone.

The National Confectioners Association reports that at least 40 percent of adults sneak candy out of the dish, and 90 percent steal from their kids! Thank God my mother wasn't a chocoholic; the good stuff was only vulnerable to swiping by my big sister. Like most kids, and not just the OCD ones, the first item on the agenda after the mission wrapped was to sort out the candy. The Casbah of trading ensued with my sister, so as to minimize the potential poaching. Then we both strategically left the "icky" stuff (translate: any marshmallowy or gummy thing, usually crusty and stale) in a place where Mom would find it. To think it would be years before I heard the phrase "win-win."

Although some point fingers at Halloween as a monstrous retail juggernaut, the centuries-old celebration has roots firmly in community. The Celtic festival of Samhain (pronounced sah-win or sow-in) probably begets the day we now call Halloween. Samhain marked the end of summer and harvest season and the beginning of winter, and always fell at the end of October. During this time of earthly transition from warm to cold and abundance to scarcity, the door between this world and the afterlife opened. Families welcomed the spirits of departed loved ones by setting out food for them, or a place at the dinner table. Bad ghosts roamed at the time, too. To confuse the evil spirits, the Celts wore costumes and masks, possibly the precursor to the Halloween costumes we don today.

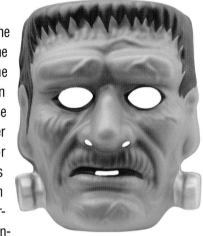

Christian influences spread through the Celtic areas and by the 8th century, the Samhain rituals had melded with the Catholic feast day, All Saints Day, on November 1. All Saints Day was otherwise known as All-hallows. Therefore, October 31st took on the name Halloween, for All-hallows Eve. The Samhain celebrations continued for centuries, with large bonfires, stories of spirits and costumes. With the influx of Irish immigrants to the United States in the mid 1800s, Halloween celebrations erupted around the country. The holiday's focus gravitated to the social and community aspects. Parties replete with games, seasonal food and costumes attracted both children and adults. By 1908, Hallmark Cards produced its first Halloween card, spawning a massive seasonal industry.

The trickster part of Halloween escalated during the 1920s and 1930s. To deal with the pranksters, many communities instituted trick-or-treating, hoping to appease the would-be mischief-makers with candy before any destruction occurred. Trick-or-treating became serious business in the 1950s and later. In a close-knit neighborhood, a kid could count on some tasty popcorn balls and maybe a candy apple. But, for most kids, their mom's warnings against the pins and razor blades hidden in such homemade treats kept them on the lookout for pre-packaged booty. I wonder, if only I had known all those years ago that the razor blade scare was a myth, how many more popcorn balls would have been mine....

With this book in hand, I can now enjoy all the popcorn balls I care to eat! And, although I'm too much of a fraidy-cat to watch a scary movie, I salute the advent of the Zombie apocalypse in the film industry, because drinking the undead on Halloween will ward off any evil spirits, as long as I only have one!

Pumpkintini

Pumpkin pie in a cocktail glass. 'Nuf said.

1 ounce vodka
½ ounce orange liqueur
1 ounce pumpkin liqueur
½ ounce Irish cream liqueur
Crushed graham crackers

Shake with ice and strain in cocktail glass rimmed with graham crackers. To rim glass with graham crackers, crush crackers in a baggie using a rolling pin. Dip rim in simple syrup and press edge of glass into crushed crackers on plate.

Zombie

This classic Tiki drink from the 1930s fits more with summer than a cool October evening, but with a name like Zombie, I couldn't resist. With the mixture of rums, more than one of these will have you looking like the walking dead the next morning. Imbibe with caution!

1/2 ounce white rum
1 1/2 ounces golden rum
2 ounces dark rum
1/2 ounce 151-proof rum
1 ounce lime juice
1 teaspoon pineapple juice
1 teaspoon papaya juice
1 teaspoon superfine sugar (or simple syrup), to taste

Mix all ingredients except 151 in a highball glass filled with ice. Float 151 on top. Garnish with a cherry and pineapple chunk.

Corpse Reviver No. 1

Several classic variations on the pre-Prohibition Corpse Reviver exist. This is the first version and possesses a darker feel than some of the other, more popular renderings.

3/4 ounce sweet vermouth
3/4 ounce applejack
1 1/2 ounces brandy or cognac

Shake with ice and strain into cocktail glass.

Spider Web Dip

This dip may seem a little hokey, but I've made it every year for my Halloween party for a long time, and there's no mystery to its disappearance.

1 can refried black beans
1 envelope taco seasoning
4 ounce can diced chiles or jalapeños, drained
1 cup salsa
1 cup sour cream
1 cup guacamole
1 1/2 cup shredded cheddar cheese
2 cups shredded lettuce
1 cup chopped tomato
Tortilla chips

Combine beans with taco seasoning and spread on a large round platter, leaving a few inches along the outside. Spread chiles on beans. Cover with salsa. Cover and smooth with guacamole. Put sour cream in a zip-lock bag and cut off one corner. Pipe concentric circles over guacamole. Draw a knife from center to outside of dip to create web effect. Layer cheese, lettuce and tomato around the outside of the dip. Put a fake plastic spider in the middle!

Chewy Popcorn Balls

Because these contain dark corn syrup and brown sugar, dying them with food coloring to make them fit your holiday event of choice isn't an option. But the darker syrup and sugar give them a wonderful caramel flavor missing from most popcorn balls. Be careful to cook only to a soft ball stage or you will get popcorn hockey pucks instead. (Boy, do I ever know!)

1/2 cup white corn syrup
1/2 cup dark corn syrup
1 cup brown sugar
1/2 cup white sugar
1/2 pound butter
1/2 cup heavy cream
7 quarts popcorn

Combine all ingredients except popcorn in a large saucepan and cook to 235 degrees (soft ball stage) using a candy thermometer. Pour over popcorn and work into balls. You might want to put oil on your hands to keep from sticking to the balls as you form them. Careful, it can be hot, too. Let set up on waxed paper.

Stuffed Mushrooms

Another classic, this recipe is so simple, don't bother buying the frozen ones at the store when you can make these in a snap.

12 whole fresh mushrooms
1 tablespoon vegetable oil
1 tablespoon minced garlic
8 ounces cream cheese, softened
1/4 cup grated Parmesan cheese
1/4 teaspoon ground black pepper
1/4 teaspoon onion powder
1/4 teaspoon ground cayenne pepper

Preheat oven to 350 degrees. Spray a baking sheet with cooking spray. Clean mushrooms. Carefully break off stems. Chop stems extremely fine, discarding tough ends. Heat oil in a large skillet over medium heat. Add garlic and chopped mushroom stems to the skillet. Fry until any moisture has disappeared, taking care not to burn garlic. Set aside to cool. When garlic and mushroom mixture is no longer hot, stir in cream cheese, Parmesan cheese, black pepper, onion powder and cayenne pepper. Mixture should be very thick. Using a small spoon, fill each mushroom cap with a generous amount of stuffing. Arrange the mushroom caps on prepared cookie sheet. Bake for 20 minutes in the preheated oven, or until the mushrooms are piping hot and liquid starts to form under caps.

Entertaining Tip:

Making it Fun with Games

If you've got the right mix of people, great drinks and food, the party will not stall. Having a couple of party games up your sleeve cannot hurt. Here's one, a form of group charades that is always a huge hit:

First, each person writes down five names of famous or infamous personalities on slips of paper. Put all slips into a big bowl. Divide the group into two teams. Set a timer for one minute, and the first person on Team A picks a slip of paper and uses words and gestures to describe the personality. Only members of Team A can guess. If Team A guesses, player one keeps the slip in Team A's pile, picks another slip and continues until the minute's expiration. A player cannot pass at any time. Team B then takes control of the bowl and does the same. After that, the second player on team A takes a turn, and then the second player on team B, and so on until all of the slips have been used. Tally each team's solved charades. All of the slips of paper go back into the bowl for round two. Use the same process as round one except a player may only use three words total to describe the personality. After all of the slips are guessed, tally correct guesses and move onto round three, in which a player can only use gestures. I still remember some particularly graphic pantomimes from a game when a few of the personalities used had become infamous for their "selfies"...

November

Spirits of Thanksgiving

Thanksgiving connotes family, football, turkey, Black Friday strategizing and dressing in funky costumes with big buckles and goofy hats. What? You don't dress up for the turkey feast day? Alas, some of us are more enthusiastic about historical costumes than others. But surely everyone can agree on those other fundamental aspects of a uniquely American holiday. At least in this century. Four centuries ago, football and Black Friday didn't exist. And no evidence proves turkey graced the first Thanksgiving table.

Family, and the larger concept of community, has remained constant throughout the evolution of the Thanksgiving holiday, however. Some experts debate the location of the first Thanksgiving, with Florida and Virginia both laying claim, but most give the Mayflower Pilgrims at Plymouth, Massachusetts the honor. Talk about community! Although documentation is scarce regarding the specifics of that 1621 feast, a few written accounts from Pilgrims give a glimpse into why and how they commemorated their first year in the New World.

The Pilgrims arrived in what is now Massachusetts in late fall 1620 after a grueling two-month sea passage. With no time to build permanent dwellings, they spent the first winter aboard the anchored and battered Mayflower. Only about half the original hundred settlers lived to see the coming spring. That small group disembarked and met, to their great surprise, a few English-speaking Native Americans. With help from the local Wampanoag tribe, the Pilgrims grew new crops and utilized the bountiful resources of sea, land and air.

After the first year, the devout Pilgrims feasted for three days, praising and thanking God for delivering them safely to the new land and ensuring a plentiful harvest.

One of the few accounts of the celebration reported they shot fowl and that their Wampanoag friends brought deer to the feast. Whether the fowl was turkey or waterfowl, like duck and geese, remains a mystery. As for the other foods they might have enjoyed, no accounts exist, but historians know the Wampanoag diet included native cranberries, as well as corn, pumpkin, and vegetables such as collards, spinach and cabbage. Without ovens or sugar, cakes or pies would have been unlikely parts of the first feast.

Similar feasts of thanksgiving occurred in Plymouth and throughout the new colonies at various times, as determined by local authorities. As the years passed, the traditional meal changed to incorporate newly introduced items, such as white and sweet potatoes. Regionally available food also differentiated celebrations between each colony. After the Revolution, several presidents, including George Washington, issued proclamations of a national day of thanksgiving. Such days often celebrated the ends to conflicts.

Mostly, a thanksgiving holiday remained a matter of a state's choice. In the early 1800s, though, magazine editor Sarah Josepha Hale campaigned to make a national Thanksgiving holiday. Unrelenting, Hale bombarded politicians for decades until finally in 1863, Abraham Lincoln declared a national day of Thanksgiving to be celebrated on the fourth Thursday of November. That tradition has continued, except for Franklin Roosevelt's attempt to stimulate shopping by moving the holiday up a week in 1939. Given current society's penchant for a great deal on Black Friday and Cyber Monday, the change seems reasonable, but the reaction in 1939 was hostile. Eventually, Congress codified in 1941 that the date for Thanksgiving would be the fourth Thursday of November.

Now, the day brings families together, making it the busiest travel time of the year. Besides enjoying a banquet of traditional foods, generations gather to watch parades and football. The traditional Thanksgiving Day parade began in 1920 in Philadelphia and was sponsored by Gimbels Department Store. A few years later, Macy's inaugurated its own parade which now ranks as the largest in the country, featuring marching bands, floats, musical performances, and the trademark spectacular giant cartoon character balloons.

The Thanksgiving Day football tradition dates back to the late 1800s when the college championship was held on turkey day. With the advent of professional football, the National Football League copied the college tradition and instituted the first Thanksgiving Day game between the Chicago Bears and Detroit Lions in 1934.

If you are like 90 percent of Americans and indulge in a roast turkey with all the fixings, and then pack the fridge with leftovers, you might need a break after a few days. Remember, you can't pick your family, but you can pick who you invite to happy hour! So extend the joy of the season with your friends and a casual night. Sit back and enjoy a cozy drink with some easy and non-turkey related appetizers.

Thirsty Jane's Nectar
This beverage was the unofficial drink of my law school softball team.
I may have thrown like a girl and swung in the wind, but I always kept the team refreshed.

1 cup unfiltered apple cider
2 ounces applejack
Cinnamon stick

Heat cider in microwave or over medium heat. Pour into a warm mug and add applejack. Garnish with cinnamon stick.

Mulled Wine
German mulled wine, called glühwein, warms revelers throughout Germany and Austria, typically during the Christmas season. Get a jump on December and enjoy some mulled wine at home in front of a cozy fire.

1 bottle red wine
1 orange
6 whole cloves
1 cinnamon stick
1/2 teaspoon vanilla extract

1 teaspoon freshly grated nutmeg
1/3 cup sugar
3 splashes brandy

Remove peel from orange with a vegetable peeler trimming white parts. Cut orange in half, squeeze juice from it and set aside. Pour about 1/4 cup of wine in a pot and add sugar, orange peel, cinnamon stick, cloves, nutmeg and vanilla extract. Bring to a boil and continue for a few minutes until syrupy. Add rest of wine, brandy and orange juice and lower to lowest heat. Don't allow wine to boil, otherwise alcohol will burn off. Leave wine to steep on low heat for about 20 minutes. Strain out spices and orange peel. Enjoy in warm mugs.

Apple Toddy

A hot toddy combines a spirit with hot water, sugar and spices. Baked apples and applejack give this version a festive fall flavor.

1 cup boiled water
2 teaspoons sugar
1 peeled, cored and baked apple (baked for 30 minutes at 325 degrees)
2 ounces applejack
Freshly grated nutmeg

Combine sugar and 1 ounce of the boiled water in a medium bowl, stirring to dissolve. Add baked apple and muddle aggressively. Add applejack and mix well. Stir in remaining water. Strain through a fine mesh strainer into a warm mug. Top with freshly grated nutmeg.

Ginger Toasts

My favorite cracker with this dip is whole wheat Melba toast. Spreading the dip on the Melba toast and garnishing with fresh rosemary creates a fancy appetizer without fuss.

8 ounces cream cheese, softened
2-3 tablespoons crystallized ginger, chopped, to taste
Rosemary sprigs
Crackers

Mix cream cheese with ginger to taste and spread onto crackers. Garnish with rosemary sprigs.

Baked Almond Brie

Fall, Brie cheese, butter, almonds and apples equal perfection. Use a spreading knife to scoop the cheese from the top. This allows the rind of the Brie to remain intact as a bowl.

1 Brie wheel
1/4 cup sliced almonds, toasted
1 tablespoon butter, cut into pieces

Place Brie on a baking sheet and put butter on top. Sprinkle with toasted almonds. Bake at 350 degrees for 8-10 minutes, until center is soft. Serve with slices of baguette and Granny Smith apples.

Sassy Saucy Meatballs

Meatballs are the go-to appetizer at my bar. Guests typically fight over the last meatball standing. Often I simply use a bottle of barbeque sauce, but sometimes I take it up a notch with this sweet and savory recipe.

1 pound frozen meatballs, heated
8 ounces cranberry sauce
5 ounces chili sauce
1 tablespoon packed brown sugar
2 teaspoons hot Chinese mustard

In a medium-size saucepan over medium heat, combine all ingredients except meatballs. Let simmer for 5 minutes, stirring often. Pour over meatballs.

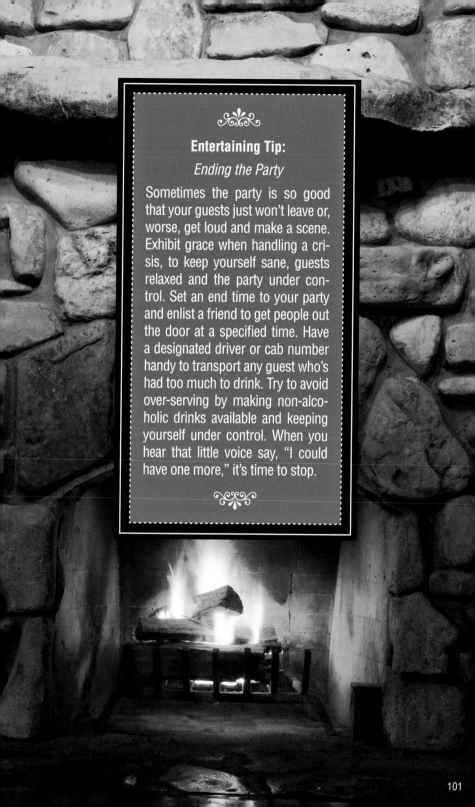

Entertaining Tip:
Ending the Party

Sometimes the party is so good that your guests just won't leave or, worse, get loud and make a scene. Exhibit grace when handling a crisis, to keep yourself sane, guests relaxed and the party under control. Set an end time to your party and enlist a friend to get people out the door at a specified time. Have a designated driver or cab number handy to transport any guest who's had too much to drink. Try to avoid over-serving by making non-alcoholic drinks available and keeping yourself under control. When you hear that little voice say, "I could have one more," it's time to stop.

December

Deck the Bar with Bubbles

Every year, the holiday party gauntlet cranks into gear as soon as Thanksgiving's turkey carcass hits the garbage can. Office parties, school mixers, social club events, neighborhood open houses, cookie exchanges and whatnot challenge us to survive December's decathlon of alcohol and appetizer overindulgence. Why do we torture ourselves so? Could it be in the name of tradition?

Like so many of our ostensible traditions, the December holiday mayhem, and specifically Christmas, isn't as traditional as we think, unless you're willing to go way back to a Roman pagan festival. And you know I am! Beginning shortly before the winter solstice (December 21st) and carrying on for a month, the Roman celebration of Saturnalia set the standard for partying. All commerce and education shut down, allowing everyone to partake in the revelry.

Early Christians did not celebrate Christmas or the birth of Jesus, but in the 4th century, the Catholic Church declared December 25th the date of Jesus' birth. The exact date of His birth is unknown. Some scholars believe the December date to be fairly accurate, but others question it and suspect that the Church chose the December 25th date to compete with, or subsume, the already established Roman Saturnalia fest. Regardless, as Christianity spread, so did the Christmas-time raucous partying.

However, with religious reform led by Puritanical forces in the 17th century, Christmas became a much more somber event, if it existed at all. British parliamentarian Oliver Cromwell actually canceled Christmas for a few years, and Christmas was outlawed in Boston for several decades in the mid 1600s.

Bah! Humbug!

Indeed, for Charles Dickens' A Christmas Carol helped resurrect the celebration of Christmas and associate the season with charity and goodwill. Americans embraced this new spirit of Christmas, and the party has been growing ever since. Well over 90 percent of Americans celebrate Christmas, even though only about half who do see it as a very religious holiday. The season is once again synonymous with revelry, as it attracts about three-fourths of all Americans to some sort of holiday party.

When it comes to partying, Champagne tops the list of the most traditional celebratory beverages. Besides being pretty, fun, and even a bit ticklish as the dainty bubbles effervesce at our noses, Champagne's royal roots give it claim as the drink for special occasions. If it sufficed for French royalty, Champagne may preside at a Thirsty Jane holiday happy hour.

Champagne is the name of a French wine region, just as Bordeaux and Burgundy denote specific areas. Beginning in the 5th century, the French court traveled to Reims, in Champagne, for coronations. At the time, quaffers consumed available local wine because transportation was not feasible and most wines lasted only about a year after production. The wines of Champagne, therefore, became the wine of royalty. The Champagne that French Medieval lords and ladies drank didn't resemble the pale bubbly delight we enjoy today. Then, local monks' vintages were still red, although pale compared to the luscious wines of neighboring Burgundy.

Fast-forwarding over a millennia to the late 17th century, improvements in the transportation system allowed vintners to ship whole barrels of wine. Sometimes, if the barrel remained sealed, the yeast in a fall-produced wine would reawaken with spring's warmer weather. When yeast consumes sugars in wine, it produces alcohol and carbon dioxide, making the wine fizzy.

Those receiving the now fizzy barrels of wine, from the royal French court in Paris to gentry in England and Holland, exhibited pleasant surprise. The popularity of the new sparkling Champagne rose because the rivers traversing its geography made shipping much easier than in other regions. At this point, an enterprising monk named Dom Perignon sought to improve the quality of his abbey's wines. Perignon's innovations include inventing the cork stopper, which allowed Champagne to be bottled in glass. He also began the practice of blending, in which several types of grapes are used to make the best wine. Finally,

Perignon removed the grape skins, which resulted in the pale white wine we now identify as Champagne.

As the wine of royalty, Champagne rose in favor with nobility around Europe. With the Industrial Revolution, however, the landed gentry no longer controlled all the wealth. A new rich merchant class arose with aspirations to acquire the same products the aristocracy enjoyed. While many could not afford Champagne for everyday use, they could spare the money for special occasions.

Now, while fine Champagne still commands a high price, other sparkling wines like Italy's Prosecco and some California sparkling wines provide excellent choices at a fraction of the cost because vintners do not use the labor-intensive *methode champenoise*, the precise way the French make Champagne. Although the best ingredients always make the best cocktails, choosing a value-priced sparkling wine for use in any of this month's happy hour drinks is perfectly acceptable and makes entertaining during an otherwise expense-riddled season affordable and, therefore, less stressful.

Another bonus to serving sparking wine cocktails at a holiday party or happy hour is that most people do not guzzle Champagne. The bubbles force the drinker to slow down and sip, which is supposedly a good way to avoid the "Champagne headache" of which some people complain. Whether you've never hosted a holiday party or the tradition is decades old, raise a glass this month to "the wine of kings and the king of wines." Cheers!

Champagne Cocktail
This classic Champagne cocktail should be mandatory before a fancy dinner. But don't save this beauty for special occasions. Its simplicity begs for frequent mixings.

1 sugar cube
2 dashes angostura bitters
1 ounce cognac
Sparkling wine

Place sugar cube in bottom of Champagne flute. Add bitters, and then cognac. Top with sparkling wine.

Entertaining Tip:

Dealing with the Aftermath

Spills happen. Glass breaks. And dishes pile up. Guests want to spend the evening with you, not see you frantically wiping down counters. Resist the urge to deep clean during a party! Instead, provide boxes to neatly collect used plates and glasses without filling the sink or cluttering the counters, and then clean everything after guests leave (or the next morning). For drink spills, try these quick emergency cleanups: For red wine, throw some salt followed by club soda on the carpet or upholstery stain and cover with a damp cloth; for juice-based cocktails, combine 1 tablespoon each of liquid dish detergent and white vinegar in 2 cups of warm water and sponge the stain with a cloth.

Sunset Mimosa

Give your mimosa a makeover by adding orange liqueur and grenadine to create a beautiful sunset sensation. Twisting the bottle, not the cork, makes opening a bottle of sparkling wine easier.

1/2 ounce orange liqueur
2 ounces orange juice
4 ounces sparkling wine
1/2 ounce grenadine

Add orange liqueur and orange juice to a Champagne flute and stir. Pour in sparkling wine. Top with grenadine.

Sparkling Ruby Punch

Punch is perfect for a holiday party because guests can serve themselves. Freeze lemons and pomegranate seeds in the decorative ice block for a cheery feel.

1/2 cup water
1/2 cup sugar
2 750-ml bottles chilled brut Champagne (or sparkling wine)
1 1/2 cups white rum
1 1/4 cups pomegranate juice
1 large lemon, thinly sliced
Pomegranate seeds
Fresh mint leaves

Bring 1/2 cup water and sugar to boil in small saucepan, stirring until sugar dissolves. Simmer 5 minutes. Cool syrup completely. Combine Champagne, rum and pomegranate juice in punch bowl. Add enough syrup to sweeten to taste. Mix in lemon slices, pomegranate seeds and mint leaves. Add ice block to bowl.

Crab Rangoon Dip

This dip appears, and rapidly disappears, annually at the neighborhood holiday party.

8 ounces of cream cheese
1/4 cup sour cream
1 can crab meat
1 teaspoon Worcestershire sauce
3 tablespoons Parmesan cheese
1/4 teaspoon garlic powder
1/4 teaspoon garlic salt

1/2 teaspoon lemon juice
2 chopped green onions

Preheat oven to 350 degrees. Mix all ingredients and bake for 30 minutes. Serve with pita chips or crackers.

Cranberry Pistachio Brie
The balsamic vinegar combined with the sweetness of the cranberries makes this dish unrivaled for a holiday party.

1/2 onion, chopped
2 tablespoons butter
1/2 cup dried cranberries
1 tablespoon brown sugar
1 tablespoon balsamic vinegar
1/3 cup chopped pistachios
1 wheel Brie cheese
1 baguette French bread, sliced

Caramelize onions in butter until golden brown. Add in cranberries, sugar, vinegar and pistachios and simmer. Melt Brie in microwave for 2-4 minutes on half power. Spread fruit-nut mixture over top. Serve with sliced French bread.

Prosciutto Fig Wraps
Rows of these little beauties lined up on a silver tray will impress your guests without you breaking a sweat.

12 thin slices prosciutto
6 ounces goat cheese, room temperature
Fig spread or jam
Arugula

Lay prosciutto flat and spread cheese over. Spread fig spread over cheese. Lay arugula leaves on top of fig spread, alternating stems and tops and allowing tops to extend about 1 inch over edge of prosciutto. Starting at short end, roll prosciutto tightly. Cut in half and stand on cut end.

Index

Who is Thirsty Jane?

Thirsty Jane is J.K. O'Hanlon, a writer, jigger jockey, equal-opportunity-boozer and former corporate lawyer (perhaps the reason for the boozer epithet?). For J.K., nothing is more satisfying than handcrafting exquisite cocktails for friends and preparing an elegant happy hour menu to complement the beverages. Yet, when entertaining the party of eight the hubby forgot to mention was coming  over, she likes to reach for something simple and reliable, like all of the recipes in this book! In addition to writing about cocktails and entertaining, J.K. is an award-winning author of steamy romances that leave readers reaching for a cool cocktail to balance the heat. When she's not mixing it up at home and/or slaving over a computer keyboard, J.K. enjoys running inappropriately long distances with her big brown dog, reading anything she can get her hands on, camping, traveling, and making friends with bartenders around the world, wheedling out recipes and secrets whenever possible. She lives in the Kansas City area, but spends as much time as possible at her second home in Puerto Rico.

Don't Leave Thirsty

Interested in getting more entertaining tips and recipes from Thirsty Jane? Sign up for her newsletter, *The Buzz*, by visiting www.thirstyjane.com. Also, like Thirsty Jane on Facebook at www.facebook.com/thirstyjane and/or follow her on Twitter @thirstyjane for free recipes and chances to win cool cocktail swag.